Receive This Light

A Play

N. J. Warburton

A Samuel French Acting Edition

SAMUELFRENCH-LONDON.CO.UK
SAMUELFRENCH.COM

Copyright © 1989 by N. J. Warburton
All Rights Reserved

RECEIVE THIS LIGHT is fully protected under the copyright laws of the British Commonwealth, including Canada, the United States of America, and all other countries of the Copyright Union. All rights, including professional and amateur stage productions, recitation, lecturing, public reading, motion picture, radio broadcasting, television and the rights of translation into foreign languages are strictly reserved.

ISBN 978-0-573-06254-4

www.samuelfrench-london.co.uk

www.samuelfrench.com

For Amateur Production Enquiries

United Kingdom and World excluding North America

plays@SamuelFrench-London.co.uk

020 7255 4302/01

Each title is subject to availability from Samuel French, depending upon country of performance.

CAUTION: Professional and amateur producers are hereby warned that RECEIVE THIS LIGHT is subject to a licensing fee. Publication of this play does not imply availability for performance. Both amateurs and professionals considering a production are strongly advised to apply to the appropriate agent before starting rehearsals, advertising, or booking a theatre. A licensing fee must be paid whether the title is presented for charity or gain and whether or not admission is charged.

The professional rights in this play are controlled by David Higham Associates Ltd, 7th Floor, Waverley House, 7–12 Noel Street, London W1F 8GQ.

No one shall make any changes in this title for the purpose of production. No part of this book may be reproduced, stored in a retrieval system, or transmitted in any form, by any means, now known or yet to be invented, including mechanical, electronic, photocopying, recording, videotaping, or otherwise, without the prior written permission of the publisher. No one shall upload this title, or part of this title, to any social media websites.

The right of N. J. Warburton to be identified as author of this work has been asserted by him in accordance with Section 77 of the Copyright, Designs and Patents Act 1988

RECEIVE THIS LIGHT

Receive This Light was originally commissioned by St Andrew's Church, Stapleford in Cambridgeshire. It was read there by Pauline Davison, Tony Porter, Peter Green and Peter Wood and directed by Kay Coe.

CHARACTERS

Woman
Man
Michael
Tom

Other one-act plays by N. J. Warburton,
published by Samuel French Ltd:

Don't Blame It on the Boots
Ghost Writer
Sour Grapes and Ashes
Zartan

RECEIVE THIS LIGHT

A bare room with one table and two chairs

Michael sits at the table, head resting on arms. Tom paces up and down. The Man and the Woman watch from outside the room— perhaps from either side of the action, or from the front, close to the audience. After a while they address the audience

Woman Petty criminals. Drifters. Nobodies. There was no reason for us to be interested in them. Except that, just then, we were in need of a nobody.
Man Our real interest was elsewhere. Someone dangerous and clever. A threat to us all in the way that these two could never be. But we couldn't get near him. Only nobodies got anywhere near him. So we needed a nobody. Otherwise . . .
Woman Otherwise we would've shown no interest in these two. We would've left them alone, to drift on, to fade completely from everyone's memory.
Man Or, of course, we would've finished with them. Completely. I mean we would've seen to it that they *didn't* drift on. Except into darkness. We had that power over them. Which they knew.
Woman Therefore we chose these two to question; to prepare; to watch unobserved.
Man And it's a funny thing but nothing gives you greater control over people than watching them when they can't see you.
Woman (*to the Man*) It's a game to you, isn't it? However serious, it's a game.
Man Yes, it's a game. We picked them up; saw a way we could make use of them. Played with them. What else would you call it?
Woman I don't know. Not a game.

Michael stirs. Tom notices and crosses to him. He slaps Michael who cringes. The Woman nods to the Man who moves into the room. He approaches Tom and Tom backs away. The Woman continues addressing the audience

It was almost certain that they didn't know our man, the one we were interested in. They were drifters so they'd probably never heard of him. Not that that mattered. What mattered was that they thought that we thought that they knew him.

She smiles and joins the others in the room, sitting at the table opposite Michael and shuffling some papers

(*To Michael*) Name?
Michael What?
Woman Name?
Michael You know my name.
Woman No, I don't.
Michael You do. I told you before.
Woman When? When have I seen you before?

Michael is confused by this and looks to Tom for help

Put it another way: I'm *telling* you I've never seen you before. So we can start from scratch. Get things clear. I like to get things clear.
Tom He can't tell you anything you don't know already.
Man Not you. We weren't asking you.
Woman (*to Michael*) You'll find it easier if we start from scratch. We can forget all the time we've wasted up to now. Talking about nothing. Getting nowhere. I don't like it when we don't get anywhere, do you? You might almost say I have an irrational fear of getting nowhere. If it is irrational. What do you think?
Michael I don't know.
Woman No. Perhaps it isn't, then. Name?
Michael You know my name.
Woman (*harder*) Name!
Michael Look, I don't know what you're after. I don't——
Man (*approaching*) How are we going to get anywhere if you won't even tell us your name?
Woman What's so secret about a name?
Man What do you lose by telling us your name?
Woman Where's the harm in it?
Man Come on, Michael. Play the game.
Woman Name?
Michael Michael. It's Michael.

Woman It'll do. For now. (*Writing*) Michael. Progress at last. Address?
Michael What?
Man You heard. Address!
Woman Where do you live?
Michael Where do I live?
Tom We can't exactly say. We're in transit, you see . . .
Man Not you. I told you before.
Woman I do see your difficulty, Michael. I'm not entirely heartless. You lock someone in a room and ask him where he lives and the logical answer must be: "Here, in this room." That doesn't get us very far, though, does it?
Man And it makes a mockery of the paperwork.
Woman Perhaps you mean "no fixed abode". Does that sound right? No fixed abode?
Michael I suppose so.
Man I suppose so, too. After all, when I picked you up you didn't look as if you had much of a home life.
Tom I can explain that . . .
Man What's the matter with you? Are you his keeper or something?
Tom No, I just wanted to——
Man Then we don't want to hear!
Tom No, you don't, do you? Ask him all the questions, keep on at him, because you can make him say exactly what you want!

The Man crosses to Tom and stares him down

Woman Oh dear. I get the impression that your friend here doesn't think you're very clever.
Michael I know. I heard.
Woman So I'll put that, shall I? No fixed abode.

Michael shrugs and she writes it down

Employment? (*Pause*) Job?
Michael I haven't got a job.
Woman Unemployed? Poor old you. (*She writes*) Now we're getting somewhere. Name: Michael. Address: no fixed abode. Employment: none. Would you say that was an accurate description of yourself?
Michael I suppose so.

Man Accurate but not exactly fleshy.
Woman Still people will draw conclusions, even from evidence as flimsy as this. You know what people are. They'll look at this and say: "I see. Feckless. Not to be trusted."
Man Scum.
Woman Which would be a pity. I mean, you wouldn't call your friend over there feckless, would you?
Man Or scum.
Michael No.
Man No, of course not. He wouldn't like that, would he? And you don't say things he doesn't like. (*He crosses to Tom and stares at him again*) Mind you, in his eyes, that's what you are.
Tom Don't listen to him, Michael.
Man I can see it in his eyes. Contempt. Oh, it may suit him to have you hanging around but it doesn't mean he likes you. You can read that sort of thing in people's eyes, you know. With a little practice you can actually see what they're thinking. I bet he can see in my eyes what I think of him.

He stares at Tom until Tom turns away

(*Smiling*) Yes. I thought so.
Tom What do you want with us?
Woman You really don't know?
Man Perhaps you should ask your friend.

Tom looks at Michael

I said your friend, not your pet dog.
Tom What friend?

Pause. The Woman stands

Woman We're interested in people, you see. It's our job. That's why we're talking to you. Let's suppose a crowd gathers, out there in the streets somewhere. We might not know why but we're interested anyway. In the crowd itself. All those people, all the destructive power, thinking as a single force. Like a storm. It swirls around and you can't tell where it's going or what it might destroy. But if you look you'll see that it has a centre. Something possibly quite still. One man, perhaps. If you can control the centre you can disperse the storm.
Man Oh yes, crowds fascinate me. I like to get inside them;

watching and listening. I see a couple of faces and I think: "Ah. Something up here. Something not quite right about these two. No jobs, no fixed abode. Scum."

Tom I don't know what you're talking about.

Man (*smiling*) I knew you were going to say that.

The Woman becomes brisk, collecting up her paper

Woman Thank you. You've been most helpful. We'll talk again later, perhaps. For now, we have enough to be going on with.

The Man and the Woman leave and assumes positions looking into the room. Tom crosses to Michael who flinches. Pause. Michael relaxes and Tom hits him

Tom Didn't I tell you? Say nothing.

Michael I didn't say anything.

Tom Oh yes? No jobs? No fixed abode?

Michael I couldn't help that.

Tom It's the worst thing you could've said. I did warn you. Several times.

Michael I'm sorry.

Tom You're sorry. That's a big help. I don't know why I bother with you.

Michael Anyway, what difference does it make? He knew everything in the first place.

Tom You didn't believe all that, did you?

Michael Why not?

Tom Because he was trying to frighten you. He won't know anything unless you tell him. (*He sighs*) They want something from us; that's obvious.

Michael What?

Tom I don't know, do I?

Michael I don't like it here. I don't like all these questions. (*Pause*) What's it like, where you are?

Tom It's not like anything. It's just a cell.

Michael I haven't got any light.

Tom So what? What do you want light for? There's nothing to do, is there?

Michael I just don't like the dark. I never have done.

Tom Oh grow up. Nothing changes because there's no light, does it?

Michael I still don't like it. It makes me feel as if they're watching all the time; as if they know all about us.
Tom I keep telling you: they only know what you tell them. (*He sighs*) And the fact that you tried to pick his pocket.
Michael Yes . . . sorry about that. I didn't realize what he was, did I?
Tom Well you should've done.
Michael I didn't actually get anything, though. Maybe he's forgotten about that.
Tom Of course he hasn't. He's just saving it up, that's all.
Michael What for?
Tom I don't know! There's something funny about all this. Why do they keep asking the same questions and then walking out, as if we've told them something?

Pause

Michael Was it true, what he said? About what you thought?
Tom Thought about what?
Michael You know . . . about being scum.
Tom Well, what do you think?
Michael I don't know. It sort of made sense when he said it.
Tom Of course it's not true. You're pig-thick and ignorant but I've got used to that. It's not the same as being scum.
Michael Why did he say it, then?
Tom It's part of his game. To turn us against each other.
Michael Is that it?
Tom Only, I don't know why. I mean, what's the point?
Michael I wish we'd never come here.
Tom Well, that's a helpful and original thought.
Michael We could've gone south. We talked about it. What do you think they'll do with us?
Tom (*tired*) Don't keep asking, Michael. I don't know.
Michael But what do you think?
Tom They could throw us out of town, I suppose. Or, if they've got it in for us, do us over and throw us out of town. But the way they've been going on, I can't help thinking they mean a bit more than that. I can't help thinking . . .
Michael (*frightened*) No. Don't. Don't say it.

The Man and Woman turn to the audience

Man You don't have to be on at them all the time. Sometimes it's just as effective to leave them on their own for a while. Especially this sort who care for nothing outside their own skins. Of course, I'd prefer not to use people like this. To my mind, a human being plays a part in society. These two have chosen to play no proper part so they have forfeited, in a sense, any claim to be truly human.
Woman (*to the Man*) You're wrong. They're people, like you and me. You may not like that but it's a fact. (*To the audience*) It would take only the slightest of changes—a twist of fortune here or there—for us to find ourselves in there, questioned and watched by them. You have to know the people you're dealing with. Know exactly what to say to them, and exactly when to drive your point home.

The Man and the Woman re-enter the room

Vagrants, petty criminals are not usually worth all this attention. It's usually best to give them a bit of a shock and then get rid of them. You, however, have become involved where you should've steered clear.
Tom Involved with what?
Man It's not simply that you are undesirable. To be frank, that was never in dispute. It's really this other business. It's political, you see, and because it's political we must be seen to act.
Tom What other business?
Man You don't worry us very much but you associate with those whose purpose is more sinister . . .
Tom Just a minute. Who are you talking about?
Man Who? This is news to you, I suppose.
Tom We don't know anyone else round here.
Woman Oh come on. We're not fencing any more. You know the man we mean.
Tom I don't. I don't know any man . . .
Woman Surely you're not going to deny it now?
Tom What do you mean? This is the first time you've mentioned anyone else.
Man No it isn't. We've mentioned him before and you raised no objections. None at all.
Tom I don't know anything about anyone!
Man Then you must be the only one who doesn't. They can't talk

about anyone else round here. To be honest with you, I'm sick of hearing about him. If it wasn't for my job I'd go straight home now and pretend I'd never heard of him. Like you.

Woman We don't want to waste time with you but you won't co-operate. All we want to know is the names of a few followers, what they get up to, what they talk about.

Tom Look, two days ago we'd never set foot here. Since then we've seen nothing and spoken to no-one but you.

Woman I'm afraid I don't believe you. If you persist in denying this cause we can only assume that you have something to hide.

Tom Will you listen to me? There is no cause!

Man But there is. We all know about it. What we want are details.

Tom From us? You said yourself: vagrants, scum. Not worth the bother.

Man That's exactly why I picked you out in the first place, friend. Our man takes a perverse pleasure in knocking around with the likes of you. God knows why.

Woman Your only value is in what you can tell us.

Tom Believe me, if I knew anything I'd tell you.

Man We've already established that we don't believe you.

Woman And you can probably see where that will lead.

Michael Where? Where does it lead?

Woman Do you really not know, Michael?

Michael Yes. You mean death, don't you? That's what you want.

Woman It's nothing to do with what we want.

Michael (*to Tom*) We can't just sit here and let them kill us.

Tom Don't be stupid. If we don't know anything we don't know anything. (*To the Woman*) What do you get out of it if we die?

Woman That's not the point. We don't get anything out of it but we have certain responsibilities.

Man I don't think they know what that means.

Tom Look, I have no objection to helping you—I'll do anything you like—but I really don't know what you're talking about.

Man And what's the difference between not knowing what we're talking about and pretending not to know what we're talking about?

Tom A very big difference to me. I can't see much future in dying, you know. (*To the Woman*) This man we're supposed to know, what's he done?

Man That's funny. We were going to ask you that.

Tom Whatever it is it gets under your skin. I can get rid of him if that's what you want. It is what you want, isn't it?
Woman We haven't said so.
Tom But it is. And you can't do it yourself...
Man We can't?
Tom Not officially, or you would've done, wouldn't you? Apart from you, no-one knows that we exist. We don't get noticed. Michael and I could take care of him for you.
Woman He dies and, as a consequence, you live? Is that it?
Tom Why not?
Woman As I said, it may not be what we want.
Tom Then, for God's sake tell us what you do want.

The Woman prepares to leave

Woman I don't wish to appear casual in matters of life and death. We'll talk about it. Later. (*She turns to the audience*) One of the pleasures of my work is when they make it sound as if it's their own idea. "Listen, listen," they say "You've got to listen to this." And they beg to do what you want them to do. You lead them to the brink of extinction, let them peep over the edge and then whisk them away again. It creates a real bond between you.

She nods to the Man who approaches the prisoners

Man All right. Tell us what you have in mind.

The Man gestures Michael and Tom out

They exit

Man (*to the audience*) You have to smile. They're prepared to do anything to stop this man; to become upright citizens for a change. They're so eager to join the fight. This place is full of people engaged in the fight. It's a warren of rooms off corridors and rooms off rooms; full of people working against threats to the way we live. Don't get me wrong. I mean threats to the way *we* live—you and me, not just me. We serve you in this, you know.

The Man exits

The Woman walks into the room

Woman Of course, we still had to take things carefully. It wasn't enough to have the man killed. The last thing we wanted on our hands was a martyr, because people remember a martyr not as he was but as they *think* he was, as they want him to be. No. He had to be abandoned and discredited. Anything short of that could have turned death into his triumph rather than ours. Which is why we needed our vagrants. Sprats to catch a mackerel. We needed them, a couple of nobodies, to befriend him ... and then betray him. (*Pause*) So we released them and, two days later, they returned—faithfully—for further questioning. (*She prepares some papers*)

The Man enters with Tom and Michael

Right. Shall we continue?
Tom If you like. What do you want to know?
Woman You've been most helpful. You've given us names, told us where he is, what he said, what happened. Now we'd like you to tell us what you think.
Tom What we think?
Woman Yes.
Tom What do you want to know that for?
Woman I'm interested. What do you make of him?
Tom He can speak to people, make them listen. It's a knack.
Woman No more than a knack?
Tom No more, in my opinion. If you ask me you're wasting your time.
Man Oh? And why is that?
Tom We've just spent two days out there following him around. We've slept out on the hillside, sat around listening to him, watched him like hawks.
Man And?
Tom We heard no plots, no threats. The man is harmless.
Woman Crowds flocked to him, you said. Isn't there a threat in that?
Tom Why? Half of them are sick or crazy. They think he can help them. He's playing on their hope, that's all. He has no power.
Woman So ... what would you do?
Tom Ignore him. Just wait for people to get fed up with him.
Woman You could be right. And what about you, Michael? What do you think.
Michael Me? Why ask me?

Woman You agree with him, then, do you?
Michael (*after a pause*) No.
Woman Go on.
Michael I think he has got power.
Man What sort of power?
Michael I don't know. Not what you mean.
Man What, then?
Michael It's sort of . . . inside.
Man Inside? What's that supposed to mean?
Michael I can't say exactly.
Man He says he comes from God, is that it?
Michael Yes . . .
Man We know this. They all say they're sent from God. (*To the Woman*) Is this getting us anywhere?
Woman What do you mean, Michael? Tell us more.
Michael (*indicating Tom*) I'm not like him. There's things I don't understand . . .
Man We noticed.
Woman Be quiet. Go on, Michael.
Michael One thing happened out there—I can't tell you exactly: it just made me think differently. After the first day we all had to sleep on the hillside and it was dark . . .
Man Dark? Night-time and it was dark? That's unusual.
Woman Listen!
Michael There was no stars. Not even a glimmer of light. I woke up . . . I thought I woke up . . . and suddenly I was afraid. Then I saw him, standing up and watching over the sleeping bodies. He had an old lamp with him. I sat up and he looked over to me. He held the lamp up. There was yellow light falling on the sleeping bodies and across the grass. He held the lamp towards me because he saw I was afraid. That's all.
Woman Did he say anything?
Michael Yes . . . but I can't remember what.
Woman And you stopped being afraid?
Michael I did.
Woman And are you afraid now?
Michael I'm afraid of this place . . . I don't like it here . . . but I understand that. It's not deep fear.
Man Were you awake?
Michael What?

Man Did this happen or was it a dream?
Michael It felt like a dream, yes. But it still happened.
Man (*to the Woman*) Is this really what we want to hear? The dreams of a half-wit?
Woman Yes. This. Exactly this.
Man Dreams? Visions? You can't make a case out of that.
Woman (*to Michael*) This made you think he *was* from God, did it?
Michael I suppose so. I don't know.
Man He doesn't know.
Michael I don't understand all this God business. I don't think about things like that.
Woman Then think about it now. What does it mean?
Tom I'll tell you what it means. It means nothing. God is an idea, that's all. An idea in the minds of the confused.
Man How profound. If we want any more philosophy we'll come to you. Till then, keep quiet.
Michael I can't tell you any more. You're supposed to be the clever ones. You tell me, because I would like to know.
Woman I know what I think. I'm interested in what you think.
Michael And I can't tell you. If I understood I couldn't tell you. I haven't got the words.
Woman Well ... We've learnt something. You've been useful, Michael.
Tom Have you finished with us?
Woman For now. But your work isn't over. You'll have to go back. One more time.
Tom And then?
Woman Then we can complete our deal and we won't want to see you again. (*Pause*) You may leave.

Tom and Michael go

Man (*to the audience*) I couldn't see the point of all this fencing. We had those two in our pockets and we were in a position to finish things off. So why did we have to tread so carefully? At times it seemed as if she didn't want to see this thing through. (*To the Woman*) What more do we need to know?
Woman A little more.
Man We're moving too slowly.
Woman We cannot rush. Things aren't quite right yet.

Man Down the corridor they are holding someone else for questioning. Not some scum picked up for the purpose. A genuine follower.
Woman Really? That's good.
Man Good? They're getting somewhere. We're not.
Woman It's not a race. We're all working to the same end.
Man Tell me why we can't finish this off now. They've got to know the man. Why can't they hand him over?
Woman You heard what the bright one said. He doesn't understand what it's all about. It doesn't mean anything to him.
Man It doesn't have to mean anything.
Woman It does. He carries no conviction. People will see right through him. Besides, there's Michael.
Man Michael? Why bother with him?
Woman He's changed. Didn't you notice?
Man How has he changed? He's just as thick.
Woman He's stopped cringing.
Man So what?
Woman It matters.
Man All right: he's changed and we're going to find out why. Let's hope it achieves something.

He leaves

Woman (*to the audience*) There was no point in jumping too soon. None of the issues was clear enough. One more time, I thought. One more time and we'll know all we need to know; we'll be in a position to act. So they went back again and, after another two days, we were ready to question them. But there was only one to ask—the wrong one. Michael had gone. (*She moves aside*)

The Man pushes Tom back on

Man Where is he?
Tom How should I know?
Man He does nothing without your say-so. Where is he?
Tom I've told you already: I don't know.
Man We were wrong about you. You're no use to us. We should've got rid of you and fumigated this place out.
Tom Really? So why worry about Michael?
Man Because I'm a worrier. Bad luck for both of us. If you had any sense you'd worry too.

Tom I did warn him, you know. I told him not to go.
Man You mean he took no notice? My word, you are losing your grip.
Tom I said you'd be bound to get him, sooner or later. He doesn't always see these things. He's not too clever, really.
Man Not too clever? He's a moron.
Tom Still, he has gone, and you haven't found him. I don't know what that makes you.

The Man slaps Tom. Pause. The Woman steps forward

Woman That'll do. (*Pause*) You can leave us now.
Man Leave you? But ...
Woman Just leave us.

Reluctantly, the Man goes

Tell me: do you know why Michael ran away?
Tom (*surprised*) Why?
Woman Yes, why?
Tom No idea.
Woman Didn't he tell you? I thought you were his friend.
Man He said he'd been feeling bad.
Woman What about?
Tom I don't know. You don't always take a lot of notice of what Michael says.
Woman You mean, you don't. What else did he say?
Tom He said ... he said he felt like a traitor.
Woman A traitor? Who to? To you?
Tom No. To our friend out there. The one we're supposed to be watching. I said that was stupid. That's why we were out there: to watch him. That's our job. If we stopped doing it we'd be traitors to you, so what was the difference?
Woman And what did he say about that?
Tom Not much. He was never over-bothered by logic.
Woman So you woke up this morning and found he'd gone. He'd gone and you stayed. You decided to remain loyal, is that it?
Tom I decided to remain alive. I'm not stupid. The odds were always slightly better if I played along with you. Besides, you're not a traitor if there's nothing there to betray, are you?
Woman Meaning?
Tom This man; there's nothing to him. He talks, yes, but none of

it's going to lead anywhere. There's no betrayal in handing over a man like that.

Woman That's not what Michael thinks, clearly. Which is rather ironic.

Tom Why?

Woman Because you're the clever one. Michael just follows. Now we need Michael because he sees something that you can't.

Tom He thinks he sees something. It doesn't mean there's anything there.

Woman All the same, we need him back. Do you think we'll get him back?

Tom You usually get what you want, don't you?

Woman Do you know where he is?

Tom No. (*A moment's pause before his betrayal*) I know where he might be.

Woman And you'll tell us where that is, of course.

Tom I could ...

Woman If?

Tom I want to be free of all this.

Woman Of course you do. And you're no use to us any more.

Tom Thanks.

Woman People wouldn't believe you. You don't carry any conviction.

Tom I get by without conviction, thanks very much.

Woman If we had Michael, you could go.

Tom I expect we can work something out, then.

Woman Good. Needless to say, I don't want to change your mind but this begins to look a little like betrayal.

She looks at Tom who hangs his head. She smiles

You buy safety, and the price is your friend. Unless friend is the wrong word. You said yourself, there's no betrayal if there's nothing to betray.

Tom Do you want my help or not?

Woman I'll guarantee safe conduct fifty miles clear of the city. After that, I never want to see you again.

Tom Don't worry. You won't.

The Woman exits

Tom stands aside with mock politeness and then follows the Woman out

A pause

The Man pushes Michael on. Michael falls. He is dirty and defeated

Man (*to the audience*) We found him where his friend said he'd be. Cowering in a hollow where a tree had fallen. Cold, hungry, snivelling. Like an animal. It disgusts me to see people sink that low. I wanted to make a quick end of both of them but she said no. Not yet. We needed Michael. And the other one? We had to let him go. Why? Because of a promise. I nearly laughed in her face. A promise? What was he that he deserved the protection of a promise? As for Michael . . .

He turns back to Michael, hauling him up and setting him on a chair

What it is to have friends, eh? I wish I had a friend like yours.

The Woman enters and approaches Michael

Woman I'm sorry to see you like this, Michael. Especially when it's so unnecessary.
Man Scared out of his wits. What little he had.
Woman *Were* you afraid? Is that why you went?
Man It hardly matters now, does it?
Woman Yes, it matters! (*To Michael*) Were you afraid of what we'd do to you?
Michael I suppose so.
Woman So you ran away.
Michael No. That wasn't the reason.
Man Then tell us the reason.
Michael I couldn't do what you wanted.
Man But you'd entered into an agreement. You *had* to do what we wanted.
Michael (*firmly*) I never agreed to lie.
Woman Who said they'd be lies?
Michael I won't do it.
Woman (*shouting*) Don't speak to us like that! I'm not asking you, Michael. I'm telling you.
Michael I can't . . .
Woman What do you mean, you can't? Who do you think you

Receive This Light   17

are? Take a look at yourself, Michael. You're broken; you've got nothing; you're completely alone. Alone. You had one friend in life and he's sold you to save his own skin.
Man (*quietly*) Stand up in court and testify. That's all you have to do. If not you'll die. Had you realized that? Endless and everlasting darkness, Michael.

Silence

Woman Your silence won't save him, you know. (*Pause*) I'll give you an hour to think about it.
Michael I don't need to think about it.
Woman Think about it, Michael! For an hour. Think about it. (*She sits*)
Man (*to the audience*) We waited. Another pointless hour. She couldn't bring herself to accept that Michael wasn't going to change; that the fear of God we usually employ so skilfully had stopped working on him. In the end, though, it really didn't matter. We heard footsteps outside, guards clattering up and down the corridors. Shouting and snapping orders at each other. Our man had been taken.

The Woman comes forward to the audience

Woman It was just as we wanted it to be. He'd been betrayed. Only, this betrayal was nothing to do with us. One of his own followers, one of those closest to him, had handed him over. Nothing to do with us.
Man I couldn't help feeling cheated; bitter at all those lost opportunities waiting around while first one and then the other became completely meaningless.

The Woman returns to Michael

Woman Oh, Michael, Michael. What difference would it have made?
Michael To me all the difference.

The Woman wipes some dirt from his face with her thumb and tries to smooth his hair

Man She always told me to understand people without getting close to them. I watched her as she said the Last Words to Michael. Not someone preparing a dumb beast for slaughter.

That's how it should've looked but it didn't. I thought: you should've heeded your own advice, woman. (*He turns and stands by the exit*)
Woman You know what must happen now?
Michael Yes.
Woman I am empowered to act for all the people. You know I have no choice in the matter?

Michael looks at her but doesn't speak

Then I am obliged to tell you that you will be removed from this place and prepared for public execution on a charge of . . . (*She hesitates*)
Man Common theft.
Woman Have you anything to say?
Michael No.
Woman You are permitted some moments in which to put your soul to rights.

She leaves

Man What a mess. And we've achieved nothing.

The Man leaves

Michael resumes the position he held at the start of the play

Tom enters and moves forward to the audience

Tom I travelled a full day without stopping, without even turning round. I set my face against the place. But there was a thought somewhere in my head that wouldn't leave me alone. It was there with every step I took away from Michael and towards safety. I cannot let him die alone. I cannot let him die alone. I stopped and shouted up at the sky. (*Shouting*) Why not? All death is alone. What's the difference if I go back? What will it matter if I'm there to hold his head at the moment of his death? He'll die just the same! Alone! (*He waits for an answer*)

Michael stands and comes forward to the audience

Michael I always had this picture in my head; a picture of my whole life like a stone road. You're walking on this stone road and it leads from birth to death. The birth is all in the brightness of day but the death is lost in darkness. You can't tell where it is.

Maybe it's only a step or two into the dark. You can't tell. Every day you walk on this stone road towards the dark. Always walking into darkness. Then there was that man on the hillside, with the yellow light all over the sleeping bodies. And it wasn't the same after that. Still walking on the same road. But the darkness ahead doesn't matter. The light is always where I'm standing. Now.

Tom (*to the audience, quietly*) Then I turned round and came back. It wasn't reason that made me do it. Reason would've kept me travelling till I was a thousand miles clear.

Michael (*turning to Tom*) You?

Tom Yes.

Michael They got you?

Tom No. (*Pause*) I came back.

Michael Why?

Before Tom can answer, the Man and the Woman return. They hold the door open at the back

Woman It's time.

Michael Both of us?

Man All three of you. You two ... with your friend out there between you.

Tom and Michael follow the Man out

The Woman watches them and then sits at the table where Michael was sitting in the first scene

Woman May God have mercy on your souls.

CURTAIN

FURNITURE AND PROPERTY LIST

On stage: Table. *On it:* papers, pen
2 chairs

Off stage: Nil

LIGHTING PLOT

No practical fittings required.

Interior. The same scene throughout

No cues

EFFECTS PLOT

No cues

MADE AND PRINTED IN GREAT BRITAIN BY
LATIMER TREND & COMPANY LTD PLYMOUTH
·MADE IN ENGLAND

www.ingramcontent.com/pod-product-compliance
Ingram Content Group UK Ltd.
Pitfield, Milton Keynes, MK11 3LW, UK
UKHW021849210426
5322IPUK00022B/555